If Forever Exists

Certain special unforgettable moments in life last a lifetime and forever seems to exist!!

If Forever Exists

Exists

The Moments That Lasted A Lifetime

RAMAN K. ATTRI

A book by Rayan & Rayman Imprints

IMPRINTS INSIGHTS

Rayan & Rayman Imprints
Rayan-rayman@outlook.com

Copyright © 2019 by Raman K. Attri and Rayan & Rayman Imprints. All Rights Reserved.

No part of this publication may be reproduced, distributed, or transmitted in any form or by any means, including photocopying, recording, or other electronic or mechanical methods, without the prior written permission of the publisher, except in the case of brief quotations embodied in critical reviews and certain other noncommercial uses permitted by copyright law. Write to the publisher/author for seeking explicit permission for any reproduction, inclusion or usage in another publication. Provide an appropriate reference/citation to this publication when posting brief excerpts or quotations from this text on social media channels. For seeking permissions to use the poems, in full or partial, in this book in any online or printed greeting cards or merchandise, please contact the publisher at Rayan-rayman@outlook.com.

ISBN: 978-981-14-1395-7 (e-book)
ISBN: 978-981-14-1394-0 (paperback)
ISBN: 978-981-14-1393-3 (hardcover)
First Published: May 2019
Cover graphics and design by Raman K. Attri
Published by Rayan & Rayman Imprints
Published in Singapore
Printed in the United States of America

National Library Board, Singapore Cataloguing in Publication Data:

Name(s): Attri, Raman K., 1973-
Title: If forever exists : the moments that lasted a lifetime / Raman K. Attri.
Description: Singapore : Rayan & Rayman Imprints, 2019.
Identifier(s): OCN 1097583333 | ISBN 978-981-14-1393-3 (hardcover) | ISBN 978-981-14-1394-0 (paperback) | ISBN 978-981-14-1395-7 (e-book)
Subject(s): LCSH: Love poetry. | Interpersonal relations--Poetry.
Classification: DDC S821--dc23

A collection of simple poems written between 1990 to 2004, translated from Hindi poetry book 'Kuch Kahi Kuch Ankahi Batein' and expanded from select English poems from the book 'Say it when You Mean it'

To Anh Chi
who showed me that "forever"
indeed exists!!

The Forever Indeed Exists by Raman K. Attri 3-May-2019

Contents

Contents xiii
The Book xix
The Author xxiii

PART 1 - THE LONER .... - 1 -

Only My Shadow .... - 5 -
Lonely as an Ocean .... - 7 -
I Need a Friend .... - 9 -

PART 2 - THE UNSAID EXPRESSIONS .... - 11 -

The Fear of Expressing .... - 15 -
To Hide the Love .... - 17 -
The One Who Lives in Me .... - 19 -
The Excuses .... - 21 -
To Say or Not to Say .... - 23 -
Silent Love .... - 25 -
My Stubborn Desire .... - 27 -

Dissipate .... - 29 -

Someday .... - 31 -

PART 3 - THE DREAM FACE .... - 33 -

Beyond My Hazy Dreams .... - 37 -

Waiting for Someone .... - 39 -

It was You All Along .... - 41 -

You're the One .... - 43 -

PART 4 - THE FIRST SIGHT .... - 47 -

When I'll See You .... - 51 -

The Girl Sitting Across .... - 55 -

My Neptune Girl .... - 57 -

What is in Your Mind .... - 59 -

Crossing Like Strangers .... - 61 -

PART 5 - THE MAGIC OF BELOVED .... - 63 -

Your Enticing Smile .... - 67 -

What You Mean to Me .... - 69 -

This Magic of Yours .... - 71 -

You're Beautiful .... - 73 -

Sensation of Her Nearness .... - 75 -

Shine of Her Face .... - 77 -

She carries .... - 79 -

PART 6 - THE LOVE HAPPENED .... - 81 -

A Thought of You .... - 85 -

If it Wasn't for Her .... - 89 -

Love Teaches ... - 91 -
Your Heartening Letter ... - 93 -
Power of Love ... - 95 -
Ever Since I've Known You ... - 97 -
Something Unknown ... - 99 -
You Mean So Much to Me ... - 101 -
I Wonder ... - 103 -

PART 7 - THE PROMISES ... - 105 -

If I Could Tell ... - 109 -
I'll Hold You ... - 111 -
If You're on My Side ... - 113 -
You'll Never Leave Alone ... - 115 -
Listen to My Heart ... - 117 -
I'm Sensitive to All Your Tears and Fears ... - 119 -
I'll Live in Your Soul ... - 121 -

PART 8 - THE DISTANCES BETWEEN ... - 125 -

I'm Always Around ... - 129 -
Missing You ... - 131 -
In Your Wait ... - 133 -
Creatures of Love ... - 135 -
Why it Happens So ... - 137 -
Find You All Over Again ... - 139 -
Is Love So Much Necessary? ... - 141 -
The Confused Emotions ... - 143 -

PART 9 - THE BROKEN HEART .... - 145 -

Heartache Unforgettable .... - 149 -

Don't Ask Me .... - 153 -

My Sorrow of Today .... - 155 -

The Poet .... - 157 -

With This Broken Heart .... - 159 -

Telling My Tale .... - 161 -

Once Again .... - 163 -

Suppressed .... - 165 -

The Irony of Love .... - 167 -

PART 10 - THE ADIEU TO LOVE .... - 169 -

Love! You Can Go .... - 173 -

Uphold Your Dreams .... - 175 -

I'll Stay Forever .... - 177 -

Reborn in My Memories .... - 179 -

Let Us Embrace and Part .... - 181 -

Time Changes .... - 183 -

PART 11 - THE MEMORIES FOREVER .... - 185 -

The Moments .... - 189 -

Memories of Childhood .... - 193 -

Memories Remain .... - 195 -

Thinking About You .... - 197 -

That Was Love, Indeed .... - 201 -

I Still Remember .... - 203 -

Still Cherish Memories .... - 205 -

Remembering You .... - 207 -

A New Beginning Again .... - 209 -

PART 12 - THE GOING BACK .... - 211 -

A Broken Star .... - 215 -

Walls of Peace .... - 217 -

Sensitive to All .... - 219 -

Becoming .... - 221 -

The Roots are Calling .... - 223 -

A Bargain .... - 227 -

Dilemmas at Every Turn .... - 229 -

Lessons of Assertiveness .... - 231 -

If We Let It Be .... - 233 -

Matter of Perspectives .... - 235 -

Call Me No More .... - 239 -

PART 13 - THE FOREVER .... - 241 -

A Timeless Desire .... - 245 -

A Continuum in Time .... - 247 -

From the Same Author .... - 253 -

The Book

The book is a collection of 89 soulful poems that reflect on how any ordinary individual feels, processes and expresses the complex emotions while reacting to the successes and failures of relationships. The poems are presented in thirteen sections, each of which represents a specific phase of the emotional journey of one's life, love, friendship, family, and relationships. Each poem is a memoir of the author's experiences at various stages of personal relationships. The poems included in this volume express a range of emotions any adolescent, young adult or grown-up feels such as love & friendship; attraction & infatuations; belongingness & loneliness; togetherness & separation; rejections & acceptances; frustrations & angers; obsessions & passion; successes & failures; confusions and reflections; heart & mind and other powerful emotions.

These poems were originally written between the year 1990 to 2004 and are published twenty-five years later in this book as a memoir to those moments. These moments, recounted through the poems in this book, stay with us forever, no matter how much we grow up in age, experience, and maturity. The book is like a time machine that would allow one to reflect back at his or her innocent times and reliving those moments again and again.

Part one: THE LONER, starts off with the poems that express what it may feel like when we are lonely, when we feel the need for a companion or when we lack a sense of belongingness.

Part Two: THE UNSAID EXPRESSIONS, represent the poems that convey a mix of emotions that we experience when we fall in one-sided love.

Part Three: THE DREAM FACE, is a collection of poems portraying what we tend to feel, imagine, hope or think about an unseen or unknown dream face who is still in our daydreams. The face, which is yet to reveal itself and keeps us on a wait clock.

Part Four: THE FIRST SIGHT, includes the expressions and reactions when we get the first sight on that 'special person' we have been waiting for years. At that moment, it seems the dream face has finally taken shape in physical form.

Part Five: THE MAGIC OF BELOVED, includes the poems expressing the magic we experience when madly in love with someone. As we know that special someone more closely, every bit of her personality appears magical and mesmerizing.

Part Six: THE LOVE HAPPENED, presents the poetic expressions that signify the wonderful and pleasant changes brought in us by the sheer sense of belongingness with someone. When we fall in love, suddenly, our whole surrounding appears to have transformed in a more meaningful way.

Part Seven: THE PROMISES, emulates the thoughts, expectations, and disappointments that arise out of promises we tend to make when we are in love. The promises, no matter broken or unkept, still tend to reside longer in memory.

Part Eight: THE DISTANCES BETWEEN, is a compilation of those poems that tells us how terrible we feel when happen to be away from our beloved ones, even if it is for a short time. Everything seems so deprived of fun and joy. All we want is togetherness as soon as we can.

Part Nine: THE BROKEN HEART, is dedicated to the unfortunate heartbreaks sooner or later everyone feels in a relationship. At that stage, everything seems so gloomy, and the end of the world appears almost as soon as tomorrow.

Part Ten: THE ADIEU TO LOVE, is an ugly inevitability that occurs in any relationship and is expressed through some heartfelt poems narrating the painful emotions one may pass through at such an emotional stage.

Part Eleven: THE MEMORIES FOREVER, represents those poetic expressions that convey that life does not stop at one place or one person. The poems in this section narrate the stage of life when seemingly inseparable people stop existing, in reality, all of a sudden and then start living in our memories and remembrances.

Part Twelve: THE GOING BACK, reminds us of a range of emotions and reactions we express toward the places we belong to, things we missed the most, the mistakes we made, friends we adored, dreams we built, failures that scared us, confusions the life brought to us. These poems remind us of the time when we wanted to run away from the present to seek a safe haven somewhere.

Part Thirteen: THE FOREVER, concludes the book with a soulful poem given to the author by one of the special souls in his life. The poem emphasizes the author's philosophy that love is timeless, boundaryless and unconditional.

The Author

Raman K. Attri is an international management consultant by profession and an engineer by background. He is not a poet by any standards or contexts. The writing was his childhood interest that he continued to pursue it in various forms and shapes. During early school and college years, he wrote verses and poetic pieces, which eventually became poems and other poetic expressions. He is engaged in transforming his previous artistic and writing work into published books that include poetry, paintings, portraits, letters, true short stories, and personal diaries.

PART 1

THE LONER

The Loner by Raman K. Attri 3-May-2019

Only My Shadow

1999

*Serene silence at this place
      my mind is still in dismay.
Feels as if I've lost my peace
      somewhere along the way.*

*A thirst so strange
      Springing up deep inside my heart.
Perhaps some ocean of love
      left behind unnoticed on my part.*

*The paths I chose, once so clear
      now are gone so astray.
Seems somehow, without knowing
      I've lost my own way.*

*Silhouette of someone's image
      forever stays with me, all the days.*

PART I – THE LONER

Feels as if my own shadow
    has left behind on some days.

Urges a silent inner voice
    to pause and wonder for a while,
See if destinations still hold the grounds
    and the journey is still worthwhile.

The image now turned misty
    once bright as a spotless glass.
Touch and see maybe just
    morning dews on the grass.

The paths once so clear
    are lost beneath the meadow.
Must be ending up on same place
    Paths many buried under the snow.

Lonely as an Ocean

6-8-1998

O! ocean!
You're just like me.
There's something common
between you and me.

Your uncharted depths
make me ponder wholeheartedly.
Perhaps, you're the one
who could understand me holistically.

Your surging waves
crashing on rocky beaches
emulates the intense desires
hidden inside my heartaches.

Why do I sense a connection,
your heart is as lonesome as mine,

PART I – THE LONER

*Miles and miles till horizon
no one is yours, nor is mine.*

*Your occasional stillness,
just like the silence my spirit bears.
Gazing over your splashes, I relived
the moments of the foregone years.*

*Your restless stormy tides
on the mere sight of the moonlight,
reminds me of my fierce desires
I harbored for someone, tonight.*

*Being beside you this moment
I'm discovering myself and I felt,
I'm not the only one lonely,
you're with me too in that 'hurt.'*

*O! ocean!
You're just like me.
There's something unknown
that connects you and me.*

I Need a Friend

9-Jan-1993

I need a friend,
*   Someone who would know,*
*   In my self-doubts,*
*   Why I'm feeling low.*
I need a friend,
*   Who could keep hope,*
*   Ask me no more,*
*   What I am going to do.*
I need a friend,
*   Preaches me no more,*
*   Someone who'd understand,*
*   What I am going through.*

Credits: Adapted from 'Say It When You Mean It' by Raman K. Attri (2018).

♥ ♥ ♥ ♥

PART 2

THE UNSAID EXPRESSIONS

Unsaid expressions by Raman K. Attri 3-May-2019

The Fear of Expressing

6-2-1993

A confession of her love, was it?
Why so mistakenly I thought.
Infinite hopes her smile kindled,
She had some interest in me, I thought.

No complaints to be told that
she couldn't see my affection.
It's me perhaps who misread
her usual smiles for other notion.

A few moments' proximities to her aura
felt as long as an infinite lifespan.
Never before I realized how life could
appear so incomplete without one.

She talked to me in such a manner,
left behind some dreams and some craving.

PART II – THE UNSAID EXPRESSIONS

Though none of her intentions,
She is my life - exclaimed heart in waiting.

Though I meant no one to her,
why I felt her like my lifeline.
Few moments her sitting next to me
felt to me as long as a lifetime.

She must have noticed my love,
after all, she does not look so naïve.
She must have reasons to avoid,
none of her faults, I sincerely believe.

Love is the strangest thing perhaps -
Until it comes, one can't survive without.
When it comes, so hard it turns to express,
Still becomes so essential in that thought.

To Hide the Love

6-1-1993

Who would speak their heart out,
If none has the time to hear?
My story won't go in a few seconds,
To narrate it'll take a long year.

I can't squander away
the pain I bear is like a treasure.
A smile on your face I want,
Anything else - I don't much care.

I wanted to scribe a tale of love -
so soulful, so unheard, so rare.
But destiny wrote a curse instead
forever for me to bear.

Now I'd stopped saying anything,
My solitude the one I'll bear forever.

PART II — THE UNSAID EXPRESSIONS

Though it suffers like a seasoned stoic,
I know I won't shed any more tear ever.

Give me the strength to hide,
deep behind my ambushes -
Those confessions and expressions,
To say once I badly needed excuses.

The One Who Lives in Me

*Everyone is smitten by her looks,
She's endearing to all like golds.
But she herself isn't aware
In whose eyes her beauty beholds.*

*Why should I search for her in nooks?
Every moment she lives in my heart.
A place she dwells every day and night,
Alas! She does not know it yet.*

*Is she really that naïve?
Or is it some kind of pretension?
In my dreamy, thirsty, longing eyes,
Why can't she see her floating reflection?*

*Calls me so lovingly and stroke my hairs,
Unaware who she torments in the dreams.
Fumes away in the haze as sunrays strike,
Open my eyes - so distant she becomes.*

PART II – THE UNSAID EXPRESSIONS

But she herself isn't aware
In whose eyes her beauty beholds.

The Excuses

11-2-1995

"I've a headache just now."
"I've some stuff to do today."
Avoid coming out with me, somehow,
She finds new excuses every day.

I might have walked her home
But she'd promise to run back home early.
I could've spoken my heart out,
had I known to make excuses so cleverly.

Perhaps I could've insisted her
To sit next to me, even if momentarily.
Only if had I gotten a chance
To gaze in her eyes pure lovingly.

A mere sight of me sometimes
Changes colors on her face in tension.

PART II – THE UNSAID EXPRESSIONS

Is she genuinely so naïve to know?
Or just some premediated pretension?

I wouldn't have fallen in love -
How to avoid, had I known how I could.
Had I known how to console my heart,
the way somehow, she always could.

To Say or Not to Say

14-4-1993

It so happens with me always
my heart forces me
to contain.
So often, I'd fallen in love -
express it or not,
the confusions prevail.
At times no one has time to listen,
then the unfinished
feelings remain.
Sometimes, I can't say everything,
sometimes, I want
silence to maintain.
Someone said, "The poet can write it all,"
but all my efforts to write
fumed away in vain.
Sometimes, I'm scared to speak out,
sometimes, it doesn't find

PART II – THE UNSAID EXPRESSIONS

the meaning to claim.
Every time I bared my feelings in love,
the fate of one-sided love
did sustain.

Silent Love

3-1-1993

When I meet with others,
I care
enough to express.
But I've
complains on myself,
to you,
why I'm so
scared to confess,
That unfortunate incomplete
one-sided love,
under demeanor shields,
I always suppress.
This went on for days,
then months,
then lost in the count of
years endless.
Now, I'm going away

PART II – THE UNSAID EXPRESSIONS

for good.
Still, grudges many
I keep
yet to redress.
Such silent
one-sided love
for you,
I forever forsake,
That I now
finally, profess.

My Stubborn Desire

11-4-1993

Fetching stars for her
- was my stubborn desire,
Making her mine
- was my constant desire.
The fire that burned
a million hearts,
Lighting the same in my heart
- was my fierce desire.

She had no time
to listen to my heart,
Still, talking my heart out
- was my foolish desire.
I did not mean much to her perhaps,
But, making her mine
- was my inconsiderate desire.

PART II – THE UNSAID EXPRESSIONS

She'd change
her path every day,
Still, waiting on every road
- was my wild desire.
She refused a million times
of her love for me,
Still, hoping her confession
- was my unfulfilled desire.

She never showered
a single smile on me,
Though, shedding tears for her
- was my crazy desire.
I tried to tell her
in a thousand ways and why,
Maybe refusing to understand
- was her stubborn desire.

She left the town
at the right moment,
Otherwise, the height of craziness
- was my mad desire.
Even after she was gone,
I kept on showing smiles
'cause hiding my grief
- was my last desire.

Dissipate

I tried not to get swayed
Why I'm still falling for her
What exactly has happened to me
A sweet feeling in my eyes linger.

I fear, in her unaware dreams
May I not remain a dream to bear.
Somewhere like a fragrance
May I not dissipate in the air.

Someday

8-8-1998

I want to ask you,
my sweet love.
If you would
recognize me one day.
Why does my love for you
goes so unnoticed?
I wonder if you would
empathize with me someday.

Like fragrance
in the breeze,
I'm afraid
I would dissipate in the hay.
Like a dream
Within your dreams.
I'm afraid,
I would shatter away.

PART II – THE UNSAID EXPRESSIONS

Come, hide me
Inside your heart,
As is your own heartbeat
Just in the same way.
So much so that
I stop existing
The way I exist today.

PART 3

THE DREAM FACE

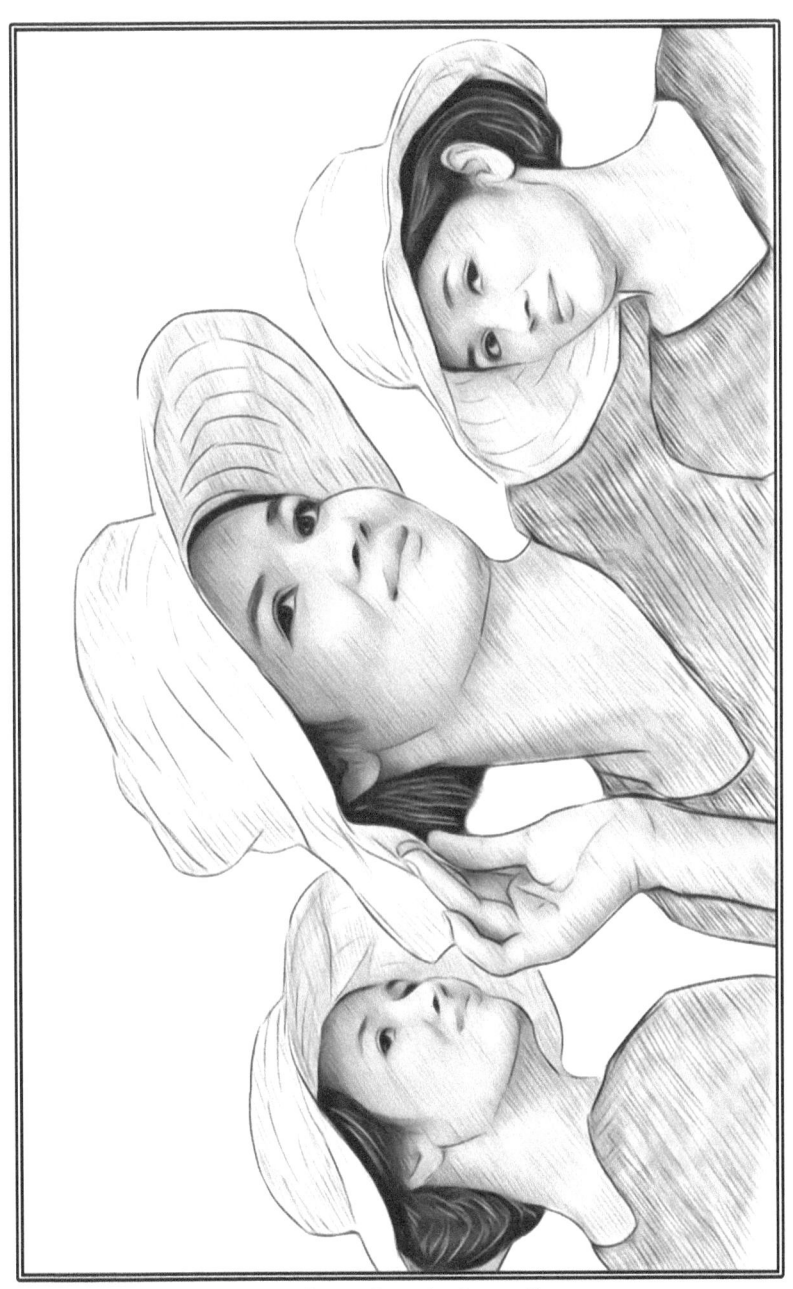

The Dream Face by Raman K. Attri 3-May-2019

Beyond My Hazy Dreams

8-8-1998

Beyond my hazy dreams,
A face lightens up often my way,
Like a ray of sunshine that emits,
Through a dark cloudy day.

Sometimes looks so familiar,
then feels like strangers on the roads.
A flash of her unknown face,
Touches my heart's chords.

There is someone, somewhere,
I'm sure who is in my wait.
Engraved as fine lines on my hand,
A name written by fate.

Behind the eyelids of her dreamy eyes,
Someone beholds a desire to meet.

PART III – THE DREAM FACE

Like a rhythmic love song,
Someone singing under the moonlight.

Seems so near, yet so far,
Around me like a fragrance.
Something is there, makes me feel
Close to me, her intimate presence.

The gust of wind stole in a whiz,
A faint scent from her body.
A sense of getting touched,
I wonder who is that somebody.

Comes in my dreams
Comes so close to me.
When I open my eyes
Fumes far away from me.

Waiting for Someone

22-8-1998

I wish I'd someone for me there -
 Beautiful bold eyes
  Carry innocence never ending;
 The glowing face
  With a thousand smiles dancing;
Her voice like a music
  The sounds tinkling bells emanating;
Guileless of her words
  A strange mischief hiding;
Through her dusky brown complexion
  A divine beauty enticing;
Deepens the cloudy sky
  With her long hair swinging;
Magic in her style
  Gives life its special meaning.

I wish I'd someone for me there -
 Humming my name unknowingly

PART III – THE DREAM FACE

With her petal-like lips;
Longing for me for ages
    Endless waiting that persists;
Wanting to hug me tight
    In her soft warm arms' grips;
The craziness of love for me
    Like a shawl she wears;
On the side of a lonely road,
    Every day she restlessly waits;
Hoping for my coming,
    With every knock on her doors;
Wishing for my one glimpse,
    That could standstill her chores.

I wish I'd someone for me there who -
    In every gust of the wind
    Who feels my fragrance that drifts;
Dreaming of me
    Middle of chilly, dark, lonely nights;
Thinking of me
    When the lively orange sun sets;
Giving knocks at my heart,
    With her own rhythmic heartbeats;
Abundance of love
    In her unique lilting, appealing smiles;
The hope of her being mine one day,
    Inducts desires to live a thousand lives.

It was You All Along

I feel "that girl" was you indeed,
Whom years upon years I waited.
Fragrance of whose body I felt so often,
As the thrush of air around me circulated.

I felt your presence through every sunrise,
I saw you in scarlet sunset at the horizons.
I've spent long and restless nights, I feel,
For you, deep in my thoughts and passions.

In my hazy dreams since adolescence,
I remember your face flashing crystal clear.
In the beats of my own heart
I know your heartbeat sounded so familiar.

I've seen this immense beauty
That your dusky complexion imparts.
I've felt the tightness of your hugs,
Embracing me with soft warmths.

PART III – THE DREAM FACE

Like tinkling of wind chimes,
I've heard your soothing voice before.
The innocence in your talks,
I'm sure I was smitten by them before.

In the depth of your dark bold eyes,
I had drowned myself a long time ago.
The incessant desire to make you mine
I feel I've possessed from the years ago.

You're the One

You're the one-
*   Whose beautiful bold eyes*
*   Carried innocence never ending;*
*   Whose glowing face*
*   Had a thousand smiles dancing;*
*   Whose voice like a music*
*   sounded tinkling bells emitting;*
*   Whose guileless of words*
*   Had a strange mischief hiding.*

You're the one -
who used to shroud my thoughts!!

You're the one-
*   Whose dusky brown complexion*
*   Had a divine beauty enticing;*
*   Magic in whose style*
*   Gave life its special meaning;*
*   Humming out my name*

PART III – THE DREAM FACE

With her petal-like lips;
Wanting to hug me tight
In her soft warm arms' grips.

You're the one —
who used to shine beyond the hazy dreams!!

You're the one-
Longed for me for ages,
With endless wait persisted;
On the side of a lonely road,
Every day who restlessly waited;
Wished for my one glimpse,
That could standstill her chores;
The craziness of love for me
Wearing like a shawl in winters;

You're the one -
who used to stand in the path of my dreams!!

You're the one-
Used to dream of me,
In the middle of chilly, dark night;
Thinking of my existence
When the lively orange sun set;
Gave knocks at my heart,
With her own heartbeat;
In every gust of breeze
My touch on your skin you felt.

*You're the one —
who used to shine in my hands as my fate!!*

*You're the one-
      Whose voice, like jingling anklets
          Made waves in my heartstrings;
The abundance of joy and love
      Your lilting laughter brings;
Giving me hope to be mine one day,
      Made me want to live a thousand lives;
Who lighted up new hopes in my life,
      Brighten up my dark inner sides.*

*You're the one —
for whom I've been forever waiting for years!!*

PART 4

THE FIRST SIGHT

The First Sight by Raman K. Attri 3-May-2019

When I'll See You

2-2-2000

Bit by bit, I collected —
some moments,
some words,
some memories,
some desires,
some dreams.

Waiting on a love —
some unknown,
some unseen,
My thoughts —
some nice, some mean,
Some naughty, some pristine.

When someone
Filled with a love infinite,
Will climb the ladder

PART IV – THE FIRST SIGHT

to my lonely heart,
Make it as her home
And live as my heartbeat.

I wanted to show
her a new world,
The world of love
Where dreams behold,
In the name of her love
As pure as gold.

That beautiful soul
will spread her scents,
In all my arts and creations
And in my talents,
Like a reborn star –
fresh and nascent.

Sketching her portrait
with love strokes,
Coloring it with
my inherent burning fires,
decorating it with
my unsaid desired.

From beyond the hazy dreams,
now you've arrived.
My beautiful love!
You've finally emerged.

Into one whole,
our hopes have merged.

More than life
I'll love you,
I'll protect you
from sorrows that spill.
Every desire that you had
I'll fulfill.

The Girl Sitting Across

26-8-1998

That girl sitting across the table,
With a special appeal crystal clear.
The breeze flowed back the scent of her skin,
That seemed astoundingly familiar.

Her lightly dusky skin-tone,
In which I saw a divine glow.
Her hazy but shining aura,
I'm sure I'd seen long ago.

Those naughty, active black eyes,
Blinking the intent to hypnotize.
On her soft, petal-shaped lips,
Flashing a smile like a sunrise.

The blows of her magical allure,
Drove infinite restlessness.

PART IV – THE FIRST SIGHT

*A charming glow on her face,
Instilled frozen stillness.*

*Touched strings of my heart,
Her steady gaze my way.
My heartbeat paused for a while,
Leaving me lifeless and in dismay.*

*She seemed to me as the reflection
of my fantasies, of my desires.
The one who has been made for me
She was the one I waited for years.*

My Neptune Girl

15-Sep-1998

What are you - Neptune girl?
A cozy, calm haven of tranquillity;
soft, dreamy and naive;
very delicate and eternally feminine;
a pretty, helpless creature;
every man's sweetheart.

What are you - Neptune girl?
Strange lights in greenish-brown eyes;
who want to see only the goods;

tiny fragile and exquisitely shaped hands;
a soft silky touch of your skin;
fine wary light hairs,
swinging over your naïve face.

What are you - Neptune girl?

PART IV – THE FIRST SIGHT

A shy smile on your lips;
but demure vulnerable to conflicts;
when reality becomes too harsh,
you hide behind your dreams.

What are you - Neptune girl?
Living in this scary world;
you carry little protection,
a cloak of sophisticated veneer;
worn to shield your anxiety
from this harsh world.

What are you - Neptune girl?
Sentimental when you're hurt,
you cry endlessly.
You pour your tender self out,
writing lovely songs and lyrics,
woven with secret messages underneath.

What are you - Neptune girl?

Credits: Inspired by Linda Goodman's Love Signs for Pisces woman. Adapted from 'Say It When You Mean It' by Raman K. Attri (2018).

What is in Your Mind

12-Jan-1993

So many persons I know
*   and so many I've seen.*
But no one like you,
*   honestly, I've ever seen.*

Sitting in a group of people,
*   still, you look distances apart.*
As if annoyed with yourself,
*   strangely detached and distant.*

Soft pinkish lips tremble to speak
*   but you nip them under your teeth.*
Your lovely eyes always lost in sleep,
*   yet, seems to be devoid of a dream.*

I don't see you waiting
*   for any special someone.*

PART IV – THE FIRST SIGHT

You have a heart beating
    which beats for no one.

You touch us like a cool breeze,
    yet, it does not belong to one.
You remind me of a wandering cloud
    that's waiting to rain on someone.

Sometimes look lost
    and sometimes trying to find.
I think of you quite often
    I wonder what is in your mind.

Crossing Like Strangers

1-Jan-1993

*I admit
I got attracted to you,
On the very first sight.*

*I urged
Talking to you for days,
And share
What's in my heart.*

*It's true
That never talked to
And we have never met.*

*Though I feel
I know you,
You don't know me yet.*

PART IV – THE FIRST SIGHT

Almost like some strangers,
Crossed each other
on the street.

Never could my eyes
Fail to tell -
How much I'm longing to meet.

So long
I've been longing
To say a few words to greet.

To Steal
Your smiles,
That makes me feel great.

PART 5

THE MAGIC OF BELOVED

The Magic of Beloved by Raman K. Attri 3-May-2019

Your Enticing Smile

1999

*The enticing smile
playing on your lips,
When loses itself
in the sorrowful ocean.
The beats that live
inside my heart,
Stop in a strange
fear yet unseen.
When your
blossoming face wilts
Even momentarily,
Then I wish
I could do something,
To bring back
your joys, instantly.
I wish I had
some special power,*

PART V – THE MAGIC OF BELOVED

To hide you
inside my soul,
From every sight,
and hurtful word,
I could save you
from every foul.

What You Mean to Me

30-9-1998

*Like fragile wings
of a butterfly,
Like untouched droplets
of morning dews,*

                                      *Such tender is
my feelings for you.*

*Like nectar
in a flower,
Like a pearl
to the oyster,*

                                      *So is your face
ingrained in my visions.*

*Like moonlight is
connected to the moon,
Like fragrance emits*

PART V – THE MAGIC OF BELOVED

from the garden,

                                So are your thoughts
                          infused deeply in my mind.

Like tides rising
from the ocean,
Like the melodies
springing out of a violin,

                               So are the desires
                         your single glimpse drives.

Like the breath
is vital for life,
Like faith
is essential for love,

                           So is the meaning you have
                             for my very existence.

This Magic of Yours

In your big deep eyes,
  Absolute truths glow and shine.
On your innocent face,
  You shower a charm so pristine.
In your melodious voice,
  I hear harmonious rhymes of a poem.
In your guileless, innocent words,
  I see strange playfulnesses chime.
In your light dusky complexion,
  An inexplicable beauty so divine.

"Do tell me! From where you bring this magic?"

Your honest, natural style,
  tells me life's bigger meaning.
On your moist pink lips,
  Several restless smiles are dancing.
The touch of your exquisite hands,
  Convey an endless craving.

PART V – THE MAGIC OF BELOVED

For someone, on the deserted paths
  Your open arms I see yearning,
Secretly wishing for someone
  As the orange sun rises in the morning.

"Do tell me! From where you bring this magic?"

Resting my head in your lap,
  Brings solace to my living.
Your hands stroking my hairs
  To me, musical notes they're playing.
Your undying faith in me,
  Gets my trust in myself soaring.
The effect of your lovely talks,
  Opens up my heart into pouring.
In your nearness, I crave,
  To live a thousand lives for loving.

"Do tell me! From where you bring this magic?"

You're Beautiful

1-Feb-2006

Your beautiful lips -
    That speak words so sweet.
Your beautiful smile -
    Fills with smile in every heart.
Your beautiful sensitivity -
    Understands everyone's hurt.

Your beautiful tears -
    Show compassion even in rift.
Your beautiful heart -
    To love you, no one can resist.
Your beautiful words -
    Who wouldn't want to trust?

Your beautiful hands -
    Everyone's desire to hold.
Your beautiful eyes -

PART V – THE MAGIC OF BELOVED

That carry depths of the world.
Your beautiful glowing face -
  A flower in the garden blossomed.

Your beautiful, magical voice -
  A pitcher of pearls creating a musical note.
The beautiful sense of belonging -
  Of being with you day and night.
Such is the beauty of my beloved -
  That no words are enough to depict.

Sensation of Her Nearness

18-9-1999

*The shine on her sweet face
as if
the moon attempts
to peek behind the cloudy hazes.*

*Smiles dancing on her lips,
as if
flowers just bloomed
in the early sun rays.*

*Her endearing words so sweet
as if
music under the moonlit night
that someone plays.*

*The magic in her voice,
as if*

PART V – THE MAGIC OF BELOVED

waves of the sea
sing a song on the shores.

The love in her dreamy eyes,
as if
through the long dark night,
a fresh morning awakes.

The sensation of her nearness
as if
a pleasant warmth that
a chilly winter fireplace imparts.

Shine of Her Face

The shine of her beautiful face
The love from her dreamy, lit eyes
Her sweet words
That Heart-touching simplicity
Her magical voice tries
That shaking smile on her lips
That feeling of her closeness

Like the moon peeking from the clouds
Like a starry night with melodies
Like someone went near the oceans shroud
Like the morning which emerges from a dark night
Like a flower blooms in early sun shines

She carries

With big deep eyes
a unique innocence she carries.
On a face that shines like moonlight
A thousand smiles she carries.
In her innocent conversations
Harmonious melodies she carries.
In her light brown color
A spiritual beauty she carries.
In her long thick black hair
Fragrance of breeze she carries.
Magic in her every move
the meaning of life she carries.

♥♥♥♥♥

PART 6

THE LOVE HAPPENED

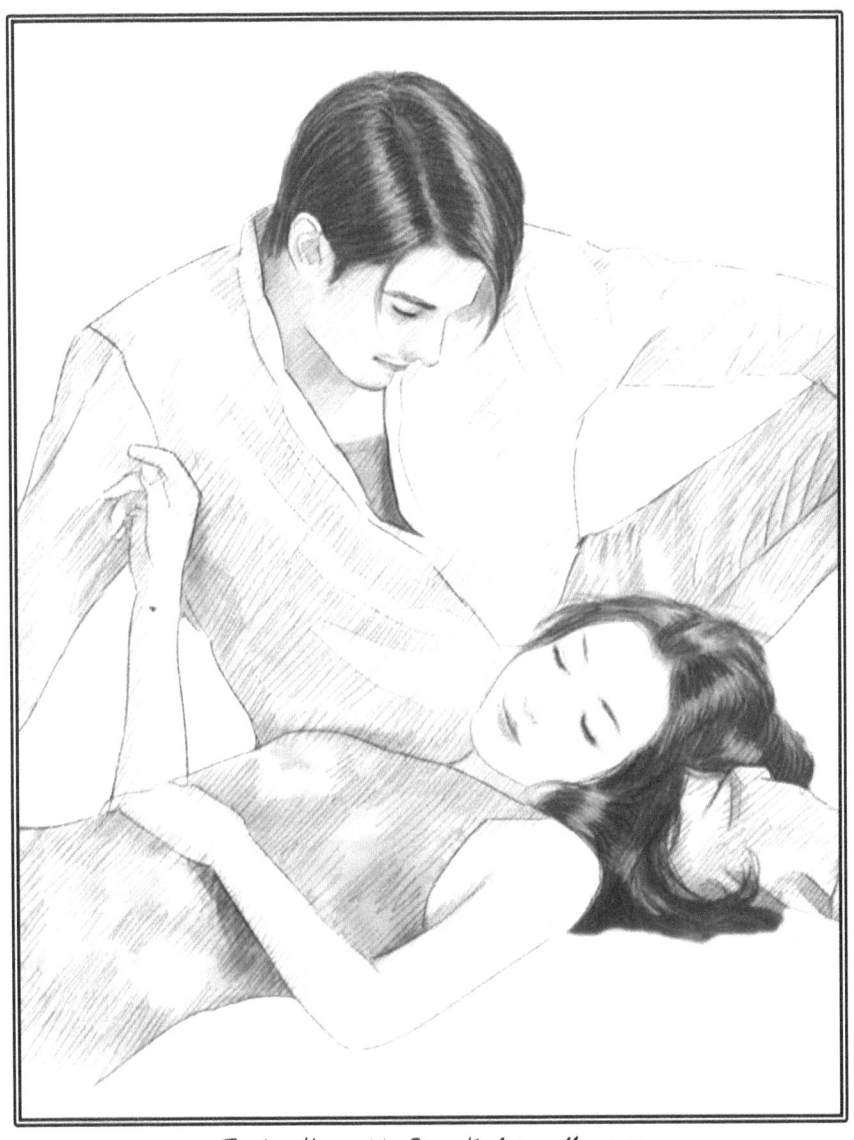

The Love Happened by Raman K. Attri 3-May-2019

A Thought of You

20-2-1993

Thought of you
makes me exhilarated
 Yet sometimes,
 life seems so incomplete.
A pleasant joy
makes me stay upbeat
 And with it,
 there is a light pinching sleet.

At times,
my heart says to get over it
 But then other times,
 I want to get lost along.
I fail to read
my own feelings,
 Drowned in this puzzle,
 Feels like, for too long.

PART VI – THE LOVE HAPPENED

What is this,
what feeling is this?
    A bit of consciousness
    And a bit reeling too.
Seems like something
might explode inside out
    And then something seems
    flowing inside too.

Heart is restless
until it sees her
    Remembering her,
    deprived of sleep at nights.
I turn anxious when
She's away sometimes,
    With each passing moment,
    She's my thoughts.

I tried hard
not to be swayed,
    Still, I don't know why
    I fell in her way.
What is happening
all over to me again?
    Sweetest feelings
    in my sighs play.

*I want to bare
all my secrets,*
  *To someone mine,
   someone close to me.
Love always feels so
I'd only heard,
   Never before was
   this known to me.*

*Why does it feel
so strange to me?
   Is it real at all?
   Or just a misconception in a blur.
Who's taken away
peace of my mind?
   Such painfully restless,
   O, heart! Never before you were.*

*Perhaps, this is
what love is all about,
   Confusion still prevails
   if it's one-sided or two.
Shall I let it be friendship
or call it love?
   A strange perplexity
   that I've fallen into.*

If it Wasn't for Her

Perhaps I'd still be living
a life of obscurity,
still, be nameless,
if it wasn't for her.
I'd have drowned
in a sea of tears by now,
if she hadn't been
standing at the shore.
Looking at her
brings peace to my heart.
It would be home to sorrow,
if it wasn't for her.
I've lost a lot
for the sake of my love.
Wouldn't have had this too,
if it wasn't for her.
Perhaps my dear ones
wouldn't have cared enough.
I'm not upset anymore

PART VI – THE LOVE HAPPENED

on losing them over her.
So close to my heart is she,
where else I'd bare my soul,
if it wasn't for her.
Life seems so fulfilled,
everything so beautiful.
It would've been a desert
if it wasn't for her.
Still would've been nameless,
not even known as a 'crazy,'
if it wasn't for her.

Love Teaches

4-1-2000

There's something in love,
even the most joyful hearts
learn to shed unstoppable tears
in the memory of their lost mates.

    Then next moment it brings a glow
    of thousand suns on the same faces.
    Teaches those sorrowful souls,
    How to burst into incessant laughs.

There's something in love,
many meanings of life, it preaches.
To forget one's existence altogether,
To discover oneself all over, it teaches.

    Never before I understood,
    these little, small, seemingly trivial things.

PART VI – THE LOVE HAPPENED

Now I've learned a mere feeling of love,
Teaches one several thousand meanings.

Your Heartening Letter

8-2-1993

I still remember,
I got your heartening letter,
tears of joy kept flowing,
making it wetter.

Before now, all that was
only in my dreams,
only in the hopes
of life's joyous streams.

Reading the letter
gave me a new feeling,
at times left me laughing,
at times weeping.

Your love inside my heart
I kept on growing.

PART VI – THE LOVE HAPPENED

How much you care,
I kept on thinking.

In it some love,
some complaints you wrote,
some love and
some desires you wrote.

Am I worth such a love?
I still can't believe.
I wonder if in return,
as much love, I can give.

Power of Love

In my heart -
I feel free;
On my dry lips -
A warm smile's dance;
In my eyes -
Heavenly confidence;
On my ugly face -
A glowing psychic light;
In my talking -
Hope of tomorrow;
In my outlook —
A positive sense about the world;
In my feelings —
A strange optimism that surrounds;
My attitude —
Is of a winner of the game;
My days -
Are full of never-ending energy;

PART VI — THE LOVE HAPPENED

In my inner self
Got over my inhibitions and fears;
Such is the power of love - perhaps.

> Credits: Adapted from 'Say It When You Mean It' by Raman K. Attri (2018).

Ever Since I've Known You

*Ever since
I've found you
beside me,
I've become more caring
somewhere
inside me.
Never was I so sensitive
to the persons
around me.
Never was the world
such a different
place for me.
Never was I so
simple to complex things
around me.
Never was I so aware
of persons so dearly
love me.*

PART VI — THE LOVE HAPPENED

*Never was I so
seeing things clearly
inside me.
Your affection is
making a beautiful
change in me.*

Credits: Adapted from 'Say It When You Mean It' by Raman K. Attri (2018).

Something Unknown

*Let there be a little enhance,
free from fear of the domestic way,
free from worries of a workday.*

*Not in the traditional way,
something is yet to appear one day,
with riddles of love, life, and joy.*

*Here in the intensity of life,
between you and me, something still unknown,
which neither you nor I can define.*

Credits: Adapted from 'Say It When You Mean It' by Raman K. Attri (2018).

You Mean So Much to Me

5-Jan-1993

You mean so much to me...
  though I hardly ever let you know.
I think of you almost every day,
  and feel your love in its rich glow.

You mean so much to me...
  for I adore the time the way, we share.
The true meaning of growing
  in the light and warmth of bond we bear.

You mean so much to me...
  when I think of the pleasant days gone by.
When I imagine about the good times yet to unravel,
  in the moments beyond today along the way.

You mean so much to me...
  I know whom to turn to and trust.

PART VI – THE LOVE HAPPENED

When I need my dearest friend,
  who will soothe me with her loving touch.

You mean so much to me that
  I would like to give you all I could.
In return for everything you gave me
  the best of everything that you could.

Credits: Adapted from 'Say It When You Mean It' by Raman K. Attri (2018).

I Wonder

9-1-1993

Once I'd insisted on having you in my life,
An unstoppable desire to make you my own.
Someday you'll come to me
— I'll wait long enough for you.

My love for you is unmeasurable,
Like the fragrances in a spring garden,
You have the right to reject if you want
— I'll still be happy for you.

In my thoughts, I'm lost and drowned,
The night is falling, and time is ticking,
I never imagined ever before that
— I'll pass my days thinking of you.

PART 7

THE PROMISES

The Promises by Raman K. Attri 3-May-2019

If I Could Tell

9-Mar-1993

How much delighted
I'll be to get you,
Your friendship, your nearness
and your love too.
How my life has changed
because of you;
If I could,
I would tell you one day.
Forget the world,
we need not to care;
They envy the love
because they don't know.
Perhaps life wants
me to come to you.
If I could,
I would tell you one day.

Credits: Adapted from 'Say It When You Mean It' by Raman K. Attri (2018).

I'll Hold You

15-Oct-1999

*I'll hold you
Until the end;
When worried,
I'll cheer you up.
When wrong,
I'll mold you.
When lost,
I'll find you.
I'll be there for you
and care enough for you.
I'll never let you part,
for you're always in my heart.
I wish
I could be there for you
when you need me.*

PART VII – THE PROMISES

I'll hold you
Until the end.

Credits: Adapted from 'Say It When You Mean It' by Raman K. Attri (2018).

If You're on My Side

19-Oct-1999

I'll take the world on stake for you.
　　I'll play the clown for you.
I'll change the rules for you.
　　Just say anything and I'll do it for you.

I told you that I need you;
　　a thousand times and why.
I played the fool for you,
　　please don't ever say goodbye.

I told you I'll get you.
　　One day will be brighter.
I'll fight with the world for you,
　　for your love for me is that would matter.

If we try together,
　　we'll not find fear or dread feeling.

PART VII – THE PROMISES

In the deepest of love,
*   once again, we will start living.*

The future we believed in
*   will reveal a joyful face.*
And the dreams we believed in,
*   will shine its grace.*

If you are on my side in this war,
*   it'll take time but one day I'll join you.*
Then there won't be any need to get hurt,
*   because so much I will love you.*

Credits: Adapted from 'Say It When You Mean It' by Raman K. Attri (2018).

You'll Never Leave Alone

17-Feb-1993

*Just call me when you can,
you will find me near every time.
Come may alone,
but you'll never leave alone.
Even if you betray,
never shall I complain,
Break your promises,
if you wish you can.
Never will I do the same,
Never leave you back again.*

Credits: Adapted from 'Say It When You Mean It' by Raman K. Attri (2018).

Listen to My Heart

1999-2000

*Whenever the wind chimes
tinkle together,
the sound that emits,
beneath those musical tones,
listen, saying to you, sweetheart -
I love you, infinite.*

*If a cool breeze
around the room
makes them chime,
be certain to hear the voice therein
listen, saying to you, sweetheart -
I want to feel you - warm and tight.*

*When the day seems
dim and sad,
listen to the calm sound,*

PART VII – THE PROMISES

it'll make you feel bold,
Listen saying in your ear, sweetheart -
hold the love for the day we meet.

Credits: Adapted from 'Say It When You Mean It' by Raman K. Attri (2018).

I'm Sensitive to All Your Tears and Fears

8-Aug-1998

*I may feel weak, hurt or emotional
but indifferent to you – never.
    Despite constant reprimands
    from your worried wears.
    I'll continue to treat
    as mine, all stresses you bear.*

*I may feel weak, hurt or emotional
but indifferent to you – never.
    Your sad saga will always make me
    spend sleepless nights.
    I'd kept my face averted,
    lest you should see my tears;*

PART VII – THE PROMISES

because I'm sensitive to all
your tears and fears.

I may feel weak, hurt or emotional
but indifferent to you – never.
    I'll try to take away the hell,
    and every day's agony you live.
    My heart will continue rejoicing
    with all your good and bad actions;
    keep on shedding tears with you,
    and consider your fears and tears as mine.

I may feel weak, hurt or emotional
but indifferent to you – never.
    If you are sad ever,
    I'll also experience the blues.
    But a song on my lips,
    just a glimpse of your face would bring.

I may feel weak, hurt or emotional
but indifferent to you – never.

Credits: Inspired by an unknown source/ anonymous work in the late 1980s. Adapted from 'Say It When You Mean It' by Raman K. Attri (2018).

I'll Live in Your Soul

25-Aug-1998

If it happened in reality
    Or it was just a dream.
I kept falling deeper into
    almost black stream;

Something strange
    Entered this surround;
I looked at the scene,
    Rubbed my eyes in astound.

In the frosty mist and twilight,
    An unearthly light was moving;
Followed by a radiant aura,
    This wonder kept on shining;

A distinguished figure of a woman

PART VII – THE PROMISES

I noticed as I gazed at it in excitement.
Enveloped in all silvery outlook,
    Of some heavenly enlightenment.

She kept coming closer and closer;
    Her face and eyes were gleaming brilliantly.
Floating and walking in the air slowly,
    Smoothly and passionately.

She looked at me with immense love,
    And at that moment I wanted to die.
What a blue shinning joy,
    Flowing out of her eyes.

It is my beloved's naïve soul
    Realizing that froze me for a while.
What a freshness and innocence
    Shone in her smile.

She raised her hands
    In careful tender motion.
And said - I came for you,
    For your obsession and passion.

If it could go on till eternity,
    I'd have loved to remain senseless.
If time could have stopped,
    My beloved's union would sustain endless.

Said she - I would stay forever,
    In your soul, in your smile shall I bloom.
Swallowed in the mist,
    She vanished into the gloom.

Credits: Adapted from 'Say It When You Mean It' by Raman K. Attri (2018).

PART 8
THE DISTANCES BETWEEN

The Distances Between by Raman K. Attri 3-May-2019

I'm Always Around

30-9-1999

Like the sky with the stars,
Like life with the breaths,

Like fragrance with the flower,
Like trust with a true lover,

        If you try, feel it, I'm always around you.

Like the light scent of your hairs,
Like the smile on your red lips,

Like dreams in closed eyes,
Like a voice tinkling in your ears,

        If you try, feel it, my presence around you.

PART VIII – THE DISTANCES BETWEEN

Like shadows resting in your laps,
Like sunshine light in wide opened eyes,

Like a warm embrace of open arms,
Like the heart that embodies the beats,

If you try, you'd know my heart is with you.

Missing You

13-7-2000

I hear your tinkling voice
In the swiftly flowing breezes.
Desiring to reach you
Like the water streams in the creeks.

Looking for your soft memories
Among unyielding rocks and stones,
Lost in your thoughts,
Pondering over distances in between.

Amidst the valleys so appealing
Still, everything appears so lonely.
Missing the times with you
Reminds me of your face so lovely.

The winds blowing over my heads,
In my ears is whispering and asking.

PART VIII – THE DISTANCES BETWEEN

Tell me - where is your beloved darling?
In this weather so pleasing.

The soft wet soil of this shore,
I try to find the scent of your skin only,
And the same loads of love,
Which I felt on your soft sweet lips only.

In the mountain and valleys,
The drip-drip of fresh morning rain,
Makes me feel so lonely,
Wondering why so long you've gone.

On the silky soft bed,
Eyes are deprived of sound sleeps.
Missing the times with you,
Searching your warm embraces.

In Your Wait

14-1-1993

From the sunrise to dusk,
From dusk to the night falls,
Counting stars in pitch-black nights,
Endlessly I wait for your short sights.

When you're not near,
How restless it makes me, dear.
The heart is also not in peace.
Without you, even time runs slower.

When you're with me,
I forget about myself and others,
Then the time turns so unfair,
Hours pass so swiftly like seconds.

Creatures of Love

1999

When you see these tiny fish,
pushing hard on the glass walls to find their way;
Think of me,
I would be restless for you too same way.

To come closer to you someday,
In the hope of the brightest day;
Think of me,
Somewhere I'd be trying hard too same way.

Waiting to get you, my dear, someday.
In the deepest oceans of love for you!
Think of me,
I would be swimming around too same way;

Credits: Adapted from 'Say It When You Mean It' by Raman K. Attri (2018).

♥ ♥ ♥ ♥ ♥

Why it Happens So

4-1-2000

Why it happens so like this in love,
the heart knows no peace without you, my love.

Your thoughts and memories every instant,
You're in my sleep, dreams, and in every breath.

Sometimes, thinking of you, my dear
My odd thoughts bring me fear.

What if one day I find you missing,
While coming near, what if you go hiding.

At times my breaths tend to stop,
A strange fear pauses my heartthrob.

I hope our love will never get cursed,
I keep asking God for blessings, untired.

PART VIII — THE DISTANCES BETWEEN

You may take even my life and my existence,
Let me with my beloved at this crescent.

Find You All Over Again

28-12-1999

Why does it happen
    That when you're far out there,
        It seems as if
        You're close to me somewhere?
Then why does it happen
    That when you're next to me,
        Still, it seems as if
        There are unbearable distances in between?
Why does it happen
    That when you're out of my sight,
        My heart wants me to
        Break all bonds and rush to your side?
Then why does it happen so
    That when I find you in my vision,
        My heart wants me to
        Find and love you all over again?

Is Love So Much Necessary?

13-1-1993

Is love so much necessary?
Neither care for the world nor of oneself,
Is being so carefree in love so much necessary?
Your sighs show suffocation,
Why are you in such a condition?
Are these sighs in love so much necessary?
This joy, this carefreeness, this glowing face,
For you, life is just another name of love,
Is being unreal in love so much necessary?
So, what if you were deceived, life isn't over yet.
Why are you so desolate on being jilted?
Is this desolation in love so much necessary?
Why do you think of the past?
You're so crazy to still wait for the one,
Is this waiting in love so much necessary?

The Confused Emotions

16-1-1993

In great happiness,
tears explode out of eyes,
In the painful sorrows,
tears run down eyes.
I was so naïve to think that
tears just symbolize pain,
They said - drenching us from within,
it's that kind of rain.

"Let's exchange our hearts."
-I often hear this thing,
I wondered if the heart was
a tangible something.
Something that resides inside,
they said in return,
Just waiting to go back
to that special someone.

PART VIII – THE DISTANCES BETWEEN

I hear everyone talking
about love, and falling in love,
I asked with my utter naivetés
- "What is this love?"
They said - it's the essence of
an unstoppable existence,
From eternity
to stay forever with persistence.

He's my friend, I'm his
– I keep hearing,
I asked them –
"What is this friendship?"
Until you need one,
we don't know what it's,
And when you have it,
then you know what bond this is,

These tears, this exchanging of hearts,
this love, this friendship,
I asked - Is it all a necessity
for being in a relationship?
They said, partly it's my misconception
and partly it's yours,
Ironically, this is one mystery
that binds us in this universe.

PART 9
THE BROKEN HEART

The Broken Heart by Raman K. Attri 3-May-2019

Heartache Unforgettable

19-4-1993

*Heartache unforgettable,
but I'll bear somehow,
The agony and the pain,
no longer I fear anyhow.*

*No one has been around me
who would really care,
The pain my broken heart
is all I have to bear.*

*Numerous times
I've agonized for others,
Yet, never had I felt nostalgic
from their self-absorbed hearts.*

The one who could belong to me,

PART IX – THE BROKEN HEART

I'm yet to discover,
I kept on searching the one,
Who could stay with me forever.

The dreams I cherished
for years broke away,
Heartaches are the ones
which always stay.

When I saw you the first time,
my heart exclaimed,
As if I found
a long-lost companion, unnamed.

Alas! Never ever you
looked at me anyhow,
And when you did,
an aloofness in your eyes I saw,

Had I sat next to you
for few moments in a stride,
But such a good fortune
never could strike.

Getting to know you intimately was
perhaps my luck overstretched.
You would remember me as a stranger,
is a hope overly far-fetched.

*I'll go on living with
your memories, deep inside,
That's the last support
On which I could've relied.*

Don't Ask Me

4-1-1993

*Talk no more
of pleasures,
It simply burns
the hearts on fires.
So unaware of what's
going on with me;
Don't ask me
whereabouts of others.
Gave me the pains
so immense;
Don't ask me
to put up sweet smiles.
Love is uncontainable
like a fragrance;
Don't ask me to hide it
beneath some lies.
Can't tell how much hurt*

PART IX – THE BROKEN HEART

I'm today;
Don't ask me
to put up a show of laughs.
The false promise you're making
to come again;
All it will lead to
an agony of endless waits.
Don't tease me
to recite a romantic poem;
Amidst the pain,
it'll merely burst me in tears.

My Sorrow of Today

My sorrow of today
I'm afraid I can't express, somehow,
Nor can I show you
The tears that I ingest, somehow.

I can't placate you,
Even if I accept my mistake, somehow.
Your smile means so much to me
Your annoyance gets on my nerves, somehow.

You mean everything to me,
Alas! I can't confess, somehow.
Probably you misunderstood me,
But I can't make you realize, somehow.

The Poet

People exclaim,
Oh! So, you're a poet!
Then you must be really
depressed from inside,
A profusion of miseries
in your heavy heart,
And desires thousands
suppressed inside.

They often say,
though there is a smile on your lips,
Your tears must be
at the verge of rolling down.
While you're so upset
with yourself,
How could you've expressed
that goes deep down?

Hear me out!

PART IX – THE BROKEN HEART

Sorrows come and go,
One who holds them
are just so naïve.
Wrapped in a
melancholy of rejection,
Did you think poets
could just only grieve?

On their lips
plays a joyous smile,
Spreading laughs
and happiness.
In the hopes to revive back
and fight with the unjust.
Not just the sadness alone
they are adept to express.

With This Broken Heart

12-2-1993

With this broken heart,
where shall I go?
Tell me, what to say to people
when they ask what I am going through?

Though many would profess
their deep love for you,
Tell me, who would love you -
The unselfish way I did to you?

Full of love for you,
You still devalued this heart.
Tell me, where shall I go
To console and pacify my hurt?

Pains of the whole world,
You have in this tiny heart,

PART IX – THE BROKEN HEART

Tell me, where shall I go –
To narrate my incomplete tale?

Everyone is being observed strictly,
No one dare to shed their tears.
Tell me, away from your alleys,
Where else could I go to hide my tears?

I'm glad my obsession for you
Rescued me with a plausible excuse,
Tell me, otherwise how else could I've
Explained this to the prying people's ruse?

Telling My Tale

2-1-1993

*What is so sickening
about this love, after all?
That people say I'm infected, above all.
You're the only cure I know of,
How on earth I could convince you so?*

*You say, go and find someone else.
Is there someone like you anywhere?
I did resolute not to let your memories play,
How on earth I make my heart obey?*

*I'm yet to see the last glimpse of my moon,
Still why eyes got filled with tears so soon.
What I should've told you rather,
How on earth I would say to others?*

Once Again

24-Mar-1993

I have fallen in love many times
Some could work, some just failed.
Every new hurt
Fetched me a new pain.
Every such pain,
Brought with it a new oath.
That never to fall in love again.

But then, I meet love again.
My resolutions get turned around.
What is right?
What is wrong?
All seems not to matter anymore.
The sweetness of newly found love,
Forgotten are the old pains.

Ready to face the end

PART IX – THE BROKEN HEART

I know it will happen again.
But then, time will
make me fall in love again.

Credits: Adapted from 'Say It When You Mean It' by Raman K. Attri (2018).

Suppressed

> I covered them,
> and I just crushed them;
> The feelings —
> I never could outburst them.
> I lived in
> a world of imagination,
> hardly getting closer
> to the realization.
> That now I'm torn
> and cannot take it anymore,
> I need a companion
> and something more.
> I want to express
> and want to share about myself,
> joys and woes of my life
> the experience of the inner self.

Credits: Adapted from 'Say It When You Mean It' by Raman K. Attri (2018).

♥ ♥ ♥ ♥ ♥

The Irony of Love

The way I tolerated your foolish hums,
And then the way of you showing tantrums,
The irony of possessiveness
Simply makes me speechless.

The way your giggling laughs echoed for me,
And then the way you screamed out at me,
The irony of mysterious emotions
Simply puts me in confusions.

The way you professed your love with heart,
And when going the way, you said you hate,
The irony of loving someone
Simply scares me from everyone.

The way you came in my life at first,
And then like a smoke how you went,
The irony of unkept promises
Simply breaks my hope for an abyss.

PART 10
THE ADIEU TO LOVE

The Adieu to Love by Raman K. Attri 3-May-2019

Love! You Can Go

31-7-2000

O love! You're all set
    To go and be free,
But remember to pass by me
    Like a gentle breeze,
Because I'll still be here
    Waiting for you in disdain,
To feel your soothing coolness
    If I could feel, once again.

Hold your hairs tight,
    Grab your scarf,
'cause if it slips off,
    I won't be around to mask.
If you couldn't do so,
    then let go loose your locks,
Feel my fingers scrolling through
    With my familiar gentle strokes.

PART X – THE ADIEU TO LOVE

Bit by bit I've assembled
 Your image on the canvas of my mind,
I am afraid you will scatter me
 Like sand slips away from the hand.
When you gaze up to the sky
 On the full moonlit night,
Don't forget to find me
 In the faintly twinkling starlight.

Words aren't enough
 To express my love so kept,
'cause tears are about to roll down
 In that vain attempt.
Sending this heartfelt letter
 Socked with tears so wet,
Knowing well that one day
 will be left to dry in your closet.

Uphold Your Dreams

31-7-2000

Neither the bonds be shackled
      Nor there be limits to our bonds.
Neither worries about any boundary,
      Nor be care of getting lost.
Neither there be any fear to embrace
      Nor be any fear to the beloved.
Complaint or annoyance, whatever may come
      I wish my beloved is never far from me.

I pray our love will always be the same
      May there be a never-ending craving to meet!
God forbids if the craving weakens ever
      May our love always sustain in the fight!
When the full moon appears,
      May you see my image in the star beside!
Even if that star isn't seen,
      May the moonlight on you forever shine!

PART X – THE ADIEU TO LOVE

Long live your dreams,
        May your all wishes come true!
Even if wishes would remain unfulfilled
        May it never break your dreams!
God forbids if broken are dreams ever,
        May sadness never break your heart!
Even if the paths seem unfamiliar
        May your directions never go astray!

Even if our directions go entangled
        May you never forget your goals!
Even if destination changes in between
        Don't be upset with life if it brings lows.
If you don't find me walking alongside
        Don't you ever feel broken and alone.
Even if you feel lonely and no one around
        May you still uphold your dreams!

I'll Stay Forever

26-8-1998

I don't remember if it's something real
Or is it an impossible dream with unreal feel.

I was drowning in the depths of oceans,
When a divine light broke through the panes.

Surrounded by a dazzling spark of light,
A miracle occurred in the misty dark night.

A silver fairy with bright, bold eyes,
I saw a woman's luminous form arise,

As if slowly floating in the air, like a cloud
I felt her approaching me in a white shroud.

In anticipation, my heartbeats almost paused
Like a gust of wind, a vibration she caused.

PART X – THE ADIEU TO LOVE

It was none other than my beloved for years I craved,
Her naïve laughter as fresh as a flower just blossomed.

A thousand hearts she could win
That kind of allure she still had within.

She held my hand in her soft, gentle hand,
Said - "I've come for your craziness unbound."

I wish that time could stand still
And I could live forever in that dazzle.

Then, came another gust of wind from afar,
Drifted away that image that rescinded in my core.

Whispered while going — "I'll not leave you ever.
In your thoughts and breaths, I'll stay forever".

Reborn in My Memories

6-4-1993

Pierced my heart with shards of separation,
I heard she's dead and went away far away,

But my naïve heart keeps iterating over,
Deep inside me she stays, how she parted way?

I'm yet to see one last glimpse of her,
How can my tears already start rolling down?
Something I couldn't even tell her,
What shall I say to the world around?

I don't know what has happened to me
I'm upset, that's what people insist.
Trying my best to laugh my way out,
Still, people say I'm desolate.

PART X – THE ADIEU TO LOVE

Today, it seems my world has changed
No laughter, no fun left anymore.
Tears are trying their best to roll,
But I'm trying hard to hold some more.

Everyone is gazing upon me,
Among this where shall I go to shed my tears for her?
My obsession for her came for my rescue,
How else I could explain what I think of her?

You say find someone to love again,
How can I find someone just like her?
What can I do when my heart not listen?
Though I promised I don't think of her.

Each time I loved, agony came to me,
I tried to laugh, only tears filled my eyes.
She died and went beyond the clouds,
But she's reborn as a star up upon the skies.

Let Us Embrace and Part

9-Apr-1993

On this last night of our relationship,
let's recall everything,
our laughs and weeps,
over the nights we spent,
dreaming of the future in our sleeps.
Let's recall
the days full of joys
and miseries we cried over.
Recall everything,
You and I can before we depart,
and then preserve those memories
in our mind for years.
You say,
let's shake hands forever,
cancel all vows taken together,
and when we may meet ever again,
we won't keep a former hatred retain.

PART X – THE ADIEU TO LOVE

Be it that we don't ignore
each other as if never met before.

Since there is no help,
come, let's embrace and part.
You don't get any more of me.
and I won't get any part of you.
We know it'll not be easy,
still, let us take our ways.
Goodbye to you
and wish you a bright life,
and thanks for so much
what you've offered to my life.

Credits: Adapted from 'Say It When You Mean It' by Raman K. Attri (2018).

Time Changes

2-Apr-1993

Time changes - come the seasons.
Everyone doesn't know the reasons.

Here comes the life and here it flies.
Here it comes in relationships and ages in years.
Passes in our acts and sustains in our memories,
The pure, rich and sweet glories.

Among those precious moments,
One day in my life is the pleasantest.
And it is the day when we met,
Reminding me of the time we spent.

There've been times we're humble,
Shared each other's anguish and trouble.
Indeed, there're the times we argued endlessly,
And teasing each other carelessly.

PART X – THE ADIEU TO LOVE

A childish fun between you and me,
A fun made up of love, affection and glee,
Which I had with you every day and night.
The memoirs I held like pearls in the oyster.

All your memories flashing on my mind this day,
I wish you the best of luck wherever you stay.
Relationships and all go through some challenges,
May destiny be cordial to you during these changes!

Time will keep on changing, coming be the seasons,
Neither you nor I'll ever know the reasons.

Credits: Adapted from 'Say It When You Mean It' by Raman K. Attri (2018).

PART 11

THE MEMORIES FOREVER

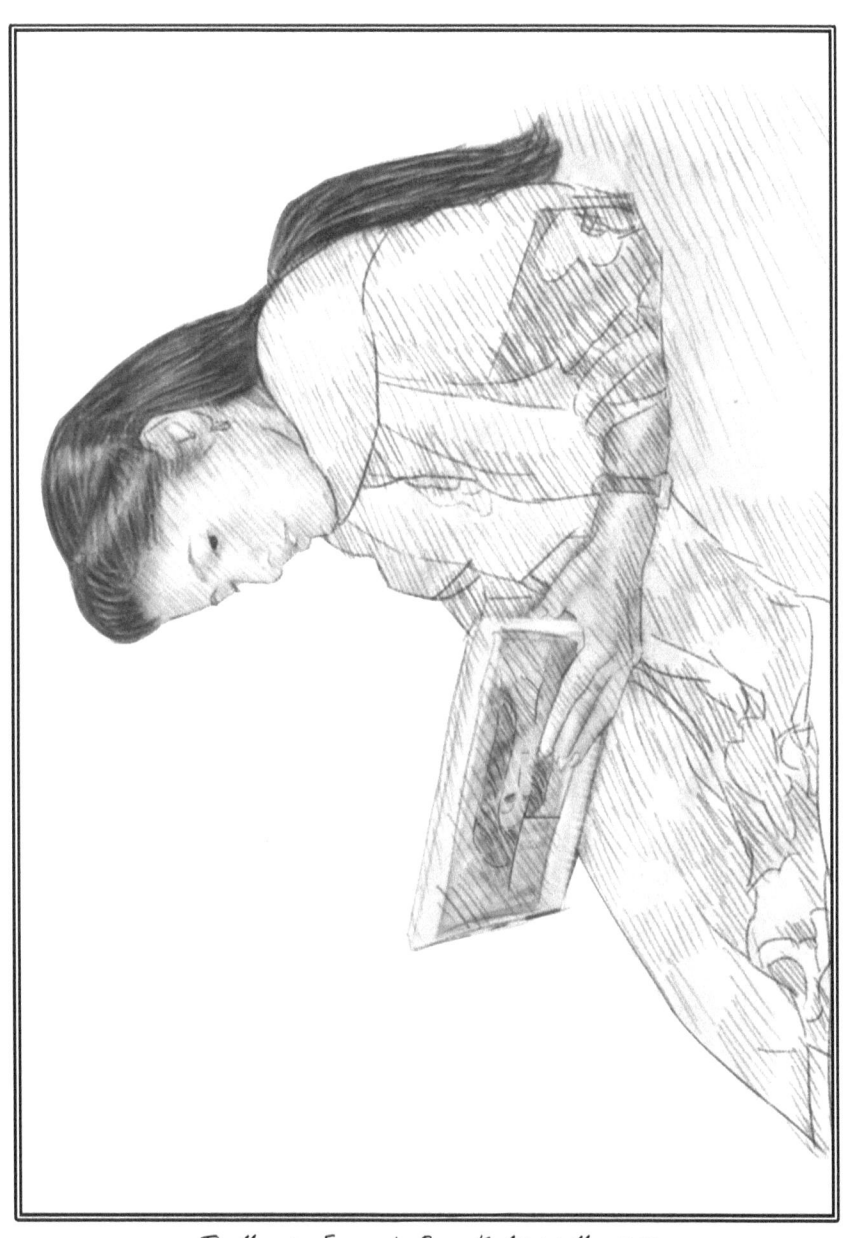

The Memories Forever by Raman K. Attri 3-May-2019

The Moments

1994

*I wish we were lost
in those beautiful moments of past,
when your soft arms
hugged me close to your heart.*

*Memories of those moments,
remembrance of experiences long gone.
Make me crave to bring you back
into my world once again.*

*When in the warmth of your arms
I'd almost forgotten myself.
Peace and calmness unfolded,
as if I came near my destiny itself.*

PART XI – THE MEMORIES FOREVER

Lost in the fragrance of your body,
as if a flower in blossoming garden.
Your presence drove in my life,
changes unsaid, inexplicable, unknown.

In the pin-drop silence,
there was a distinct echo of our heartbeats,
as if a harmonious song of rhythm
Sung between your and my heart throbs.

The silence between you and me
for years, I saw slowly getting faded.
Turning gradually into stormy emotions,
God knows since when we'd harbored.

I wish if I'd some powers
to command the time to stop.
Putting a hold on day's movement
and telling night to halt.

We wouldn't have to wait for a year
for this one day to come back.
Neither the time would've changed,
nor I'd gone so restless in your wait.

Today, the same moments came back,
we've the same love flourishing all over.
I feel your nearness once again
and sensation of you being mine forever,

*No other desire in life remains
but an unstoppable thirst,
for your closeness in the years to come
and for your love in the quest.*

Memories of Childhood

7-8-1998

Those beautiful memories of our childhood
    And among them is her face,
        And on that lovely face
            A tiny cute smile,
                At times used to shine for me.

Busy in the dreams of tomorrow
    Those dreamy eyes of her,
        Movement of her hands,
            Almost like wings of a bird
                Ready to fly, she used to tell me

A fantasy her words implied,
    To create a new world of her own,
        Out of her daydreams,
            Break free of all the bonds
                the desires she shared with me.

PART XI – THE MEMORIES FOREVER

Her sneaking out to meet me
    And be absorbed talking to me for hours,
        Getting lost thinking about tomorrow
            Used to make me go restless
                Her sitting so close to me.

Holding my hand in hers
    Showed her faith in me,
        So long it took me to understand
            Her desire to fly away
                Not alone but soaring with me.

Memories Remain

9-8-1998

Hands in hands,
  Eyes gazing into mine,
    Your sweet shyness,
      And blinking of your eyes,
        All those moments
          are still alive in my memory.

For the first time
  When I kissed your soft lips,
    The effect of their nectar
      I feel till date on my lips,
        All those moments
          are still alive in my memory.

In those rainy days,
  Thinking of your nearness,
    The scent of your body

PART XI – THE MEMORIES FOREVER

I still feel in my breathing,
All those moments
are still stay in my memory.

Thinking About You

24-8-1998

Lost in each other, forgetting everything else,
Days have passed since we sat together.
Years and years have gone in the air since we shared
The happy-sad moments that we spent together.

Those precious enrapt moments
When love carried at times a tint of annoying,
That innocent mischief of childhood
There was a strange joy even in sulking.

Amidst our families' bickering
We swear over and over, never to meet again.
And the next very moment
We sit on the terrace hand-in-hand again.

Bursting into laughter like a spring
When seeing me after long times.

PART XI – THE MEMORIES FOREVER

And then your sea-like deep eyes
Shedding tears while telling me your tales.

Experiencing the joyful chores,
Uncountable years we have spent.
Flourished the flowers of our desires,
More than today, all the hopes that meant.

In my reflections of those times
You bring some joy, and then some griefs.
The reminiscence of your thoughts storm,
As if wind sweeps load of autumn leaves.

I feel I've come too far ahead of time
In search of something, in life's race to find.
Your thoughts strike me sometimes as if
A treasure perhaps I've forgotten behind.

The life full of confusions
Rare are finding the bonds of care.
My heart desires over and over
If you're near me somewhere.

While being away from you,
I've seen a truly unexpected in the fog.
Rarely was that away from me
What I searched around the globe.

You were the one
heard my soul crying behind my walls.
Without any said words
You could tell me about my heart's calls.

Come, let's run away far away
Away from the chaotic sighs,
Let the layers of the heart open up
Under such beautiful skies.

That Was Love, Indeed

7-2-1993

*How lovingly
you used to call me,
How your gaze conveyed
a longing for me.
Never before I felt things
This way,
The love you
showered on me.*

*I'm weird, and
a little mad too,
Maybe you can call me
a bit crazy too.
Have been searching
for love every corner,
Hardly I recognized
it was so near.*

PART XI – THE MEMORIES FOREVER

*Hardly did I understand
The words behind your silence,
Your touching, your hugging
and your affection.
I failed to see
the sparkles in your eyes,
Never could I understand
 those loving gazes.*

*Though you've been with me
for a long before,
Why life never seem
so beautiful to me before.
Missed seeing the love
you had hidden tactfully,
The love you're showering
all the while so selflessly.*

*I don't know how long
I yearned for such love,
Now let me forget
all that loneliness in your love.
The seas of silent love
that resided in you all the time,
Let me get drowned in
those oceans for some time.*

I Still Remember

10-1-1993

Your meeting, your parting,
I still remember,
Your coming to me,
And then going away,
I still remember.

Your getting annoyed,
Your turning upset,
My cajoling you,
Still your showing egoism,
I still remember.

Your blushing,
your stuttering in anticipation,
Your professing your loving,
I still remember.

PART XI – THE MEMORIES FOREVER

Your promises,
Your swearing,
You have the right to forgetting,
but I still remember.

Your laughter,
your smiles,
Your giggling still echoes
In my ears - I still remember.

Those days are past,
those nights won't return,
Yet the love still remains,
I still remember.

Beautiful were those moments,
Such an alluring life with you,
The memories of those moments,
I still remember.

There was a lot to be said,
These eyes will speak,
A rain untold held in them,
I still remember.

Still Cherish Memories

10-Feb-1993

It's true we're miles and miles apart.
Still, often I remember you in my thought.
    Life is hard and tough at times,
      What we tackle day and night.

Sometimes we're helpless,
And sometimes lost for a while.
    On every such a moment,
      I wanted so much to talk to all the time.

I wished to see you,
but I couldn't come your way.
    I wished to write to you,
      But something came on my way.

Now so many persons I know
but nobody like you I've seen.

PART XI – THE MEMORIES FOREVER

I've come to realize that
To each other, how much we mean.

It was never obvious to me,
Until the day we parted our paths.
   With all your fun and charm,
   Let's try to relive our past that we lost.

I hope you'll forget that has gone,
And would be back to me once again.
   With a newness in our relationship,
   On the grounds of a new understanding grown.

Credits: Adapted from 'Say It When You Mean It' by Raman K. Attri (2018).

Remembering You

29-Jan-1993

It has been a while we sat together,
and shared the joy and woes together.

The times of warmth and care,
sweet were those gone yesteryears.

I embrace the memories of those times,
Still, I relive those precious moments.

I still remember those days,
when we lived the moment of enjoys.

Sometimes I get excited and gloomy sometimes,
when we shared ideas and thoughts so fine.

I wished to write to you day and night,
but something wasn't in favor of mine.

PART XI – THE MEMORIES FOREVER

It is true we are now far apart,
you've to believe, I did not forget you all this
while.

How can I forget you, so good friend of mine?
Hope you'll forgive me and good to me again.

Credits: Adapted from 'Say It When You Mean It' by Raman K. Attri (2018).

A New Beginning Again

We really had the moments of joys,
When we indulged in long talks for hours.
    Sometimes annoyed with each other,
    And sometimes teasing each other.
Waiting eagerly to see and talk together,
Moments of loving and caring for one another.
    At times when we ignored each other,
    Still so memorable the days we had
    together.
It has been a while we sat together,
And shared the joys and woes together.
    I wish we could have lived longer together,
    Perhaps it would've made a different world
    altogether.

Credits: Adapted from 'Say It When You Mean It' by Raman K. Attri (2018).

PART 12
THE GOING BACK

The Going Back by Raman K. Attri 3-May-2019

A Broken Star

20-8-1998

My heart often asks to go back
  To the 'paradise' once I cherished.
Where I'd harbored a desire to fly up high
  Like a free hummingbird.

The walls of that hostel
  Calling me to come back.
Back to where I felt connected
  With everything and every nook.

An untrodden path in the meadows,
  So apt to recognize my footsteps.
Strange music played
  Humming wind against trees and stems.

That tiny room of mine
  Wrapped the whole universe inside.

PART XII – THE GOING BACK

Gifted me with thousand experiences,
    Thoughts and ideas to pride.

My beloved's pictures all around,
    As if she'd come to life at any moment.
A feeling of warmth surrounding
    Drenched in her body's faint scent.

The whole world's joys I'd gathered,
    There was a peace, a heavenly solace.
I'd put together a thousand dreams,
    Life seemed so sweet to face.

Maybe I'd left something behind,
    Perhaps subdued love of boyhood.
All those fun-filled friendships,
    Some deep – some misunderstood.

The open sky shining with a full moon
    Used to embrace with her open dark arms,
Beneath it, I'd nurtured a desire
    To shine up high alongside twinkling stars.

I wish I could go back in time,
    And ponder on my destiny once again.
Why I ended up being a broken soul,
    In an attempt to make my name.

Walls of Peace

20-8-1998

Lost in the world of happy thoughts.
If I'd stayed in that place for a while longer.
At least I would've not seen
My dreams broken and shatter.

Slept at my will, woke up as I wished.
Rapt in myself, unaware of others whatsoever,
At least I wouldn't have been woken up
In the middle of the nights in terror.

Far away from these worries
Content in myself, no pain to tremor.
At least I wouldn't have
Ended with this feeling of being a loser.

If someone had told me that time to treasure,
I wouldn't have crossed the fences over.

PART XII — THE GOING BACK

*I wish time could've stopped there and then,
And I would've lost in time somewhere forever.*

Sensitive to All

8-Mar-1993

I cannot blame anyone,
For the fault lies within me.
It's no one's problem but mine
If I let people hurt me.
I cannot hold it against anyone,
For being what they are.
Trample on my feelings
And let people hurt me.
It includes my friends,
Because they matter.
And so are their actions and words,
Their fears and tears,
Their successes and failures.
I am sensitive to everything of theirs.
Why do you let things affect you?
Why don't you just ignore them?
Despite constant reprimands

PART XII – THE GOING BACK

from my worried well-wishers,
I continued to treat,
As if mine, were the problems of theirs.
Because someone's sad saga
Had me spent sleepless nights.
And someone else's pain and anguish,
haunted me for a long.
I felt their hurt as if it was mine,
And share the hell in which they live
But I go about my day,
Letting every little thing bother me.
I also experience the blues,
If sad are the people around.
And someone's happy smiling face,
Brings a song to my lips.
But sometimes I ponder -
Does all this matter to them at all?
In this world of make belief,
Good intentions are not appreciated.
And thoughtful gestures are laughed at
But my tender inner declared -
I will continue to rejoice
to their failure and successes,
Shed tears with them,
And listen to their fears.

Credits: Adapted from 'Say It When You Mean It' by Raman K. Attri (2018).

Becoming

22-9-1998

*Long bred expectations haunt me
Of being someone worthwhile.
In the crowd of ordinary people,
I'll do something in distinctive style.*

*I wanted to run swiftly
Faster than time ever could.
To a world full of fun
To feel all the joys unbound.*

*Surpassing ordinary successes,
To write a new history.
I came here with such hope,
To make a new identity.*

*The way some light tower gives
A faint hope to ships searching for the banks.*

PART XII — THE GOING BACK

Same hope resided me in long enough,
Keep me pushing through the cranks.

But time showed me the mirror
Thrown me as an ordinary man in a swarm.
Sense of destinations have faded,
Like a sinking boat in the storm.

Even though,
long bred expectations still haunt me
Of being someone worthwhile.
In the crowd of ordinary people,
I'll do something in distinctive style.

The Roots are Calling

23-8-1998

O wind!
Tell the soil of that city,
That its fragrance I still remember.

That little house,
better than bungalows on the seaside.
The rooftop of that house
Where I nurtured wishes to fly up and wide.
Behind those walls
my few desires are still embedded inside.

O wind!
Go and tell that house,
That I still remember
The moments spent under its protective ceiling.

PART XII – THE GOING BACK

Those neighborhood's friends
with them, some little plays unfold,
Those trivial disputes
Still full of naïve naughtiness cajoled.
Those people of the street
Spreading an exceptional warmth untold.

O wind!
Tell the people of that city,
That I still remember
The childhood's tiny little lovely memories.

The classes at my first school,
Where my real childhood nurtured intensely.
That banyan tree in the middle of the playground,
The shade of which still soothe me occasionally.
Those adorable classmates,
Used to discuss their heart out profusely.

O wind!
Tell the plants and trees of that school
That I still remember
The times I'd spent beneath.

My childhood's beautiful friend,
With whom I wove some fantasies, some dreams,
Some tender naïve moments,
She and I shared talking about our kidding plans.
Her sneaking out hiding from others

To talk her out from dusks till dawns.

O wind!
Go and tell that girl,
That I still miss the naïve talks
I'd with her for years.

That second school,
And my first love of adolescence,
From the corner of my longing eyes,
I endlessly admired her innocence.
A thousand letters I wrote to tell
But never could even once.

O wind!
Go and tell my first love,
That I'm still in love
With the glimpses of her decade after.

That city where I grew up,
The streets and roads that belonged to me.
The lonely bridge over the dried up river
Standing and perhaps waiting for me.
Those seemingly inanimate lifeless things,
Usually used to talk to me.

O wind!
Go and tell that city,
That I still remember

PART XII – THE GOING BACK

Each lifeless thing in it gave me a special life.

That girl, that first love,
That school, and those classmates,
That house, those friends,
That city and its crossroads,
Living in those are my memories
And some unforgettable episodes.

O wind!
Go and tell them all,
That I still remember
Miles away but adore every bit of connection I still have.

A Bargain

20-4-1993

What is real,
what are the games?
This confusion
I never understood so far.
Whom to trust?
And who to leave -
That fine divide
Never could I draw.

The turns life brings
Are so confusing.
Seems so true sometimes,
so fake in the next.
A fine line between
truth and lie
never could I decide.

PART XII – THE GOING BACK

In the bargain of love
I lost my life.
For a stranger
I gave up all I'd.
In the wish
To make her my own,
Those who called me their own.
Never could I keep.

Each time I tried
To laugh with others,
Only tears rolled down
my longing eyes.
Living in a hell
With suppressed desires.
Why don't those desires die?
Never could I find.

I took the thorns
of sadness and sorrow,
I showered my joys
and delights on others.
Each time I fell in love,
Heartbreak was the only prize.
Not let them take me for a toll
Never could I stop.

Dilemmas at Every Turn

5-1-1993

We create confusions,
We then resolve troubles,
After sorting out these ravels,
We get invaded by new puzzles.

While solving the puzzles,
We get drowned deeper,
In these self-construed problems,
Sometimes we can escape never.

If we do escape from the nuisance
We adopt new complications.
We tend to go after the trivial,
then tend to run away from obfuscations.

Sometimes we're ahead of complexities,
At times the intricacies trap us.

PART XII – THE GOING BACK

Wrapped up in these complexities
Long life just passes by us.

When life reaches its end,
A new dilemma spring up,
Wondering what we achieved in life
In that perplexity, life ends up.

Lessons of Assertiveness

29-Aug-1998

You may not have listened me say it too often,
That unconsciously, you've taught me a lesson;

The lesson of realities and truths untold;
The crimpled frailties of life, a heart can't hold.

The expression of anger from words to practice;
The art of genuine agitation against injustice;

With you, I understood why one must have arrogance;
When treated badly by people after you were gone.

Forgiveness work sometimes, bygones are not gone.
One must push back unjust criticism and put-downs.

Art of being assertive, fighting back and stand;
For our rights, feelings, freedom, and demand.

PART XII – THE GOING BACK

Your bubbling zeal for achieving greater success,
 I feel is the essence of life for its fullness.

Your rare art of living life lively and being cheerful;
 Gives me a ray of inspiration to be joyful.

Credits: Adapted from 'Say It When You Mean It' by Raman K. Attri (2018).

If We Let It Be

11-4-1993

Joy and sadness are strange feelings,
No one gives you nor it comes from outside.
These big and small things of life,
Appear the way you think inside,

Sometimes feels so real, sometimes like a lie,
Life is a feeling that rises deep inside.
If we feel it deeply, heart goes in pain,
If we sense it, beautiful the life feels instead.

Someone's rejection can break hearts,
But then other times it seems so trivial.
The heart does not get flustered from big obstacles,
But then little things can put us on trial.

This sadness, pain or betrayal
Sometimes may seem disheartening,

PART XII — THE GOING BACK

If we approach it with a positive mind,
None of that seems too prolonged standing.

Matter of Perspectives

20-4-1993

Autumn comes,
Leaves will fall off the trees,
No matter where.
So will be the spring,
It will blossom the gardens,
No matter where.
A matter of place and timing,
Seasons will come,
no matter where.
Some will blossom,
Some will fall,
no matter where.
It's just a matter of perspective.

Sometimes the 'time' follows us,
Sometimes we feel as 'puppets.'
It's a matter of a chance,

PART XII – THE GOING BACK

no matter where.
Some would fall sometimes.
Some would miss sometimes.
It's just a matter of perspective.

Dreams are fragile,
But hold perpetual longings.
Some will fill the hearts with joys
When they come true.
Some will fill us with pain
When they get shattered.
It's just a matter of perspective.

There will be turns in life
Some moments will be sad.
Some will lead to joys
Beyond today's grief.
All this is part of a journey,
Sometimes we will stop,
Sometimes we will ride.
It's just a matter of perspective.

Who will be with you?
It's a matter of fortune.
Some will extend their hands,
Some will walk away.
How we feel in a moment?
It's just a matter of perspective.

Thousands of people we meet,
Some like strangers
Some like our own.
Some will pretend to love,
Others will betray us.
It's just a matter of perspective.

All the lamps are meant to lighten,
Some will be burned out,
Some will still burn bright.
Some will brighten us,
Some will dampen.
It's just a matter of perspective.

Call Me No More

16-Feb-1993

Call me no more from the past,
No more give me the gloomy cast,
The thoughts I don't want to adopt.
To the time that is lost.
Yet remain some faint impressions on the track
Often trying to drag me back.
Cling no more to what's gone,
The things which had driven me insane.
Long gone is who I was,
Give me no more songs so sad.
Forgot all that didn't matter again,
No hatred no grudged to retain.

Credits: Adapted from 'Say It When You Mean It' by Raman K. Attri (2018).

PART 13

THE FOREVER

The Forever by Raman K. Attri 3-May-2019

A Timeless Desire

1-12-2000

*Each time I found my reflections
in her deep ocean-akin eyes,
I just used to ponder sometimes –
What if this ocean had a shore somewhere!
That would've been better, perhaps.*

*Each time her memories strike,
Tears rolled down my eyes unstoppably.
I used to ponder sometimes –
What if I'd not fallen in love with her!
That would've been better, perhaps.*

*Each time I found dark clouds of loneliness,
shrouding my shiny days,
I just used to ponder sometimes –
What if you had been near me!
That would've been better, perhaps.*

PART XIII – THE FOREVER

Each time I recalled reminiscence of
moments spent with her,
I just used to ponder sometimes –
What if those days could return back!
That would've been better, perhaps.

Each time I found myself alone,
I just used to ponder sometimes –
What if you were my loneliness!
That would've been better, perhaps.

> Credits: The Hindi version of this poem sent by Neeru H on Dec 2000; the original authorship/source of the poem is unknown. The author is indebted to the original poet for writing so great lyrics – an ideal end-note for this book.

A Continuum in Time

The front and back covers of this book connect two worlds of one's life — on a continuum of time — what we want and other is what we really need as we traverse through complex emotions of life and relationships. The back cover is a snapshot in time back then that represents my deeply rooted attractions, dreams, and desires, once so dear that I hoped for them to last forever. The front cover denotes those experiences and realities which I now hope must last forever. More often those are the experiences that makes us believe that "forever exists."

Perhaps...
Forever Exists
Somewhere,
In Some Realm.

Front cover art

When Dreams Become Reality
by Raman K. Attri
30-April-2013

Back cover art

Face of the Dream
by Raman K. Attri
7-Aug-1998

Artworks credits

Front cover artwork: When Dreams become Reality, painted in the year 2013
Back cover artwork: Face of the Dream, painted in the year 1998
All the inner sketches, portraits and illustrations by Raman K. Attri, 2019
Front and back cover art by Raman K. Attri
All artwork copyrights © 2019 Raman K. Attri

From the Same Author

Say It When You Mean It: *Poetic Expressions by A Non-Poet*
Published: 2018
Collection of poems in English
ISBN 978-981-14-0827-4 (ebook)
ISBN 978-981-14-0828-1 (paperback)

Kuch Kahi Kuch Ankahi Batein: *Timeless Untold Expressions (Hindi Version)*
Published: 2019
Collection of poems in Hindi
ISBN 978-981-14-0826-7 (ebook)
ISBN 978-981-14-0825-0 (paperback)

Expressions Untold – Moments Unfold: *Timeless Poetry (Roman Hindi Version)*
Published: 2019
Collection of poems in Roman Hindi
ISBN 978-981-14-0823-6 (ebook)
ISBN 978-981-14-0839-7 (paperback)

Available at major retail and online stores
Write to rayan-rayman@outlook.com to place the order